a guide for t̲

john m. vitek

Living

the

Questions

Jesus

Asks

Saint Mary's Press
Winona, Minnesota

Genuine recycled paper with 10% post-
consumer waste. Printed with soy-based ink. 50572

The publishing team included Steven Roe, development editor; Laurie Berg-Shaner, copy editor; Barbara Bartelson,
production editor and typesetter; Cären Yang, designer;
Andy Palmer, cover designer; cover photo by Jane Weis-
brod/Imageworks, Inc.; manufactured by the production
services department of Saint Mary's Press.

The acknowledgments continue on page 114.

Printed in the United States of America

Printing: 9 8 7 6 5 4 3 2 1

Year: 2010 09 08 07 06 05 04 03 02

ISBN 0-88489-782-6

Library of Congress Cataloging-in-Publication Data

Vitek, John.
    Living the questions Jesus asks : a guide for teens / John
M. Vitek.
        p. cm.
Includes index.
    Summary: Twenty-six challenging, prayerful, and life-af-
firming reflections for Catholic teens seeking a deeper un-
derstanding of their faith.
ISBN 0-88489-782-6 (pbk.)
    1. Catholic youth—Prayer-books and devotions—Eng-
lish. 2. Jesus Christ—Teachings—Meditations. [1. Prayer
books and devotions. 2. Catholic Church—Prayer books
and devotions.] I. Title.
BX2198 .V58 2002
248.8'3—dc21
                                        2002010851

Living
the
Questions
Jesus
Asks

Contents

8   Introduction

16   Who do people say that the
     Son of Man is?

20   Where is your faith?

23   What do you want me to do for you?

27   What does it profit them if they gain the
     whole world, but lose . . . themselves?

31   What were you arguing about
     on the way?

35   If you lend to those from whom you
     hope to receive, what credit is that to
     you?

39   Which of these . . . was a neighbor?

42   Do you see this woman?

46   Why do you see the speck in your
     neighbor's eye, but do not notice the log
     in your own eye?

49   Why do you ask me about what is good?

53   Who will give you what is your own?

57   What do you think?

60   Are you envious because I am generous?

63   And can any of you by worrying add a
       single hour to your span of life?

67   Who is my mother, and who are my
       brothers?

70   Is there anyone among you who, if your
       child asks for bread, will give a stone?

74   Does he not . . . go in search of the one
       that went astray?

77   What are you arguing about with them?

81   Who touched me?

85   How long has this been happening
       to him?

88   What is your name?

92   Were not ten made clean? But the other nine, where are they?

95   Why are you sleeping?

99   If you love those who love you, what reward do you have?

103   Why are you afraid?

106   When the Son of Man comes, will he find faith on earth?

109   Topic Index

Introduction

The questions Jesus asked the people of his day were life-changing questions. They were questions that got people's attention, made them pause, think, and answer—and, then, commit themselves to a new way of life.

The questions Jesus asked others over two thousand years ago are the same questions he asks each of us today!

Many of the questions Jesus asks are the same ones you may have asked yourself or others. The questions Jesus asks are common sorts of questions, like "Why are you afraid?" and "What are you arguing about?" He also asks some personally challenging questions, like "Why do you see the speck in your neighbor's eye, but do not notice the log in your own eye?" His questions are often quite blunt and to the point; for example, "Are you envious because I am generous?"

Jesus expected those of whom he asked questions to answer in their own words and from their heart, even though he had a clear sense of what the answer ought to be. For instance, after telling the story of the good Samaritan, he asks, "Which of these was a neighbor?" The somewhat obvious answer is "the Samaritan." But what confused the people of Jesus' day was how someone from another community, an "outsider," could be a neighbor. Is this still confusing today? Jesus wants you to think about the question and search your heart before answering. In this case he wants you to know what it means to truly be a neighbor (see "Which of these . . . was a neighbor?" on page 39).

In other words *Living the Questions Jesus Asks* is for all of you who are seeking answers to life's big questions.

Within the pages of this book, you will find answers to such timeless questions as these: Who is God? Who is Jesus? Why should I believe in Jesus Christ? What does it mean to believe in Jesus Christ? What does it mean to live a Christian life? How am I to treat others?

Living the Questions Jesus Asks is for all of you who believe deeply in Christ and his message, as well as for those of you who are uncertain about your belief or about your desire to come to a deeper knowledge of Christ and his message.

If a warning label could be applied to the cover of this book, it might read: "Caution! Answering the questions Jesus asks may change your life, forever!" Following the way of Christ in the world is simple—love the Lord your God and love your neighbor as yourself—but doing these "simple" things is far from easy. Jesus expects a radical commitment from you, as you will discover through the questions he asks. This means that he calls you to follow him completely, which requires aligning your whole heart, your whole mind, and all your actions with the will of God. It's that simple—and yet it's not that easy. This book, then, is meant to be a help along the way to encourage you, to inspire you, to give you pause, to help you think about the things that matter most in life, and to help you find meaningful answers to life's big questions.

You may find that as you read this book you will want to talk with others about your faith. Take a risk and do so. The Christian life ought to be shared with others in community, not lived in isolation. So talk with others about your questions, about Jesus' questions, about the answers you hear in your own heart and mind, about what the Church teaches. Talking with others about what you read in this book is one of the surest ways to come to greater clarity and peace in your mind and heart.

Living the Questions Jesus Asks contains twenty-six chapters, one chapter for each of Jesus' questions. Within each chapter you will find five sections: Jesus asks you, search your mind, hear your tradition, commit your spirit, and pray your heart.

Jesus Asks You

At the start of each reflection is an actual question that Jesus asked, as recorded in the Bible. Following the question is an excerpt from the Bible showing the wider context in which Jesus asked the question. You may wish to have a Bible on hand to look up the passage so you can read the entire chapter or more.

Search Your Mind

Each question that Jesus asked is recast in this section as if Jesus were asking you the question today, which he is. This section offers some thoughts for reflection on Jesus' question and some ways it has been answered by others. The important point to remember in this section is that you are being challenged to answer Jesus' question in your own way.

Hear Your Tradition

Have you ever asked, "What does the Church teach about this topic?" This section provides a brief comment on what the Church believes, related to Jesus' question and his message. Catholic Christians believe that God's word is revealed through both the Bible and Tradition—the living transmission of the Good News of Jesus Christ through the Church. Many of the quotes you will read in this section come from the *Catechism of the Catholic Church (CCC)*, a compendium of Catholic doctrine.

Commit Your Spirit

One of the main teachings of Jesus and the Church is that words of belief are not the whole story. Following the message of Jesus Christ requires both word and deed—professing and living your faith. This section offers some simple ideas to help you commit yourself to living your faith in everyday life. The suggestions are often simple, but not necessarily easy.

Pray Your Heart

The final section of each chapter offers words that invite you to pray. The prayers are intended to help you open your heart and mind to the message of

Jesus and the Church. Faith is a gift, freely given by God to those who seek it and open their heart and mind to God's grace. So don't forget to pray for what you seek.

At some point while reading this book, or perhaps after you've finished reading it, you may have questions or comments of your own. If you would like to, please e-mail your questions or comments to me at *jvitek@smp.org.* I'd be happy to hear from you.

God be with you as you ponder the questions Jesus asks, and may we all have the courage to follow the way of Jesus Christ, which is the way of truth and life. Peace.

John M. Vitek

John M. Vitek
President, Saint Mary's Press

Jesus

ASKS YOU

"Who do people say that the Son of Man is?"

¹³Now when Jesus came into the district of Caesarea Philippi, he asked his disciples, **"Who do people say that the Son of Man is?"** ¹⁴And they said, "Some say John the Baptist, but others Elijah, and still others Jeremiah or one of the prophets." ¹⁵He said to them, "But who do you say that I am?" ¹⁶Simon Peter answered, "You are the Messiah, the Son of the living God." ¹⁷And Jesus answered him, "Blessed are you, Simon son of Jonah! For flesh and blood has not revealed this to you, but my Father in heaven."

—Matthew 16:13–17

Search Your Mind

If Jesus met you on a street corner today and asked, "Who do you say that I am?" how would you answer? Would you describe Jesus as a great person who once lived? Would you describe Jesus as a great prophet? Would you describe Jesus as the Son of God, true God from true God, the Savior of the world?

For Christians, Jesus is far more than just a historical person who lived a holy life. He is the Christ, the "anointed," the Word of God made flesh, our Lord and Savior. He has perfectly revealed God's intention for the world and how we are to live our lives. He continues to be among us through the Holy Spirit, leading us and teaching us the way to eternal life, happiness, and fulfillment. He is the way, the truth, and the life. To follow Jesus is to follow the will of God, the Father, the Creator of all that is good.

Who do others say that Jesus is? Do you ever talk with your friends about who Jesus is? Do you ever talk about Jesus' significance in your life and in the life of the world?

Hear Your Tradition

"We believe and confess that Jesus of Nazareth, born a Jew of a daughter of Israel at Bethlehem at the time of King Herod the Great and the emperor Caesar Augustus, a carpenter by trade, who died crucified in Jerusalem under the procurator Pontius Pilate during the reign of the emperor Tiberius, is the eternal Son of God made man." (*CCC*, no. 423)

Commit Your Spirit

Sometime in the next day or two, commit yourself to having a conversation with at least one of your friends. Ask your friend, "Who do you say Jesus is?" Let this conversation be a time when you openly talk with each other about your belief in Jesus. Consider making a commitment with your friend to talk each week about your belief in Jesus and your questions of faith.

Pray Your Heart

Help me, Lord, to know more deeply who you are in my life and in the world. I ask that my mind, my heart, and my thoughts be opened to whatever you wish to reveal to me. For this I pray. Amen.

Jesus

ASKS YOU

"Where is your faith?"

²²One day he got into a boat with his disciples, and he said to them, "Let us go across to the other side of the lake." So they put out, ²³and while they were sailing he fell asleep. A windstorm swept down on the lake, and the boat was filling with water, and they were in danger. ²⁴They went to him and woke him up, shouting, "Master, Master, we are perishing!" And he woke up and rebuked the wind and the raging waves; they ceased, and there was a calm. ²⁵He said to them, **"Where is your faith?"** They were afraid and amazed, and said to one another, "Who then is this, that he commands even the winds and the water, and they obey him?"

—Luke 8:22–25

Search Your Mind

Where is your faith? In what or whom do you place your faith—your trust and belief? If you were caught in the middle of a great storm or some other kind of danger, would you place your trust in God? This passage evokes the story of Cassie Bernall, a student at Columbine High School, in Colorado, who, when a fellow student was about to pull the trigger of a gun to kill her, was asked, "Do you believe in God?" She said, "Yes." In the face of death, she proclaimed that her faith was in the Lord. Would you have done the same?

Hear Your Tradition

"Fear is a fundamental affection, or feeling, of the human person. In itself fear is neither good nor evil. Fear can be morally good when it contributes to good actions, but morally evil when it contributes to actions that are contrary to God's will." (Adapted from *CCC*, nos. 1771–1773)

Commit Your Spirit

At times in your life, you will face a dangerous or frightening situation. When you encounter those moments, you will have to make a choice: to give in to your fear or to place your faith and trust in the Lord. Commit yourself to placing your faith and trust in the Lord, and repeat these words: "Lord Jesus Christ, I place my trust in you."

Pray Your Heart

Lord, in moments of danger or fear, I need you to help me remember always to place my faith and trust in you. Help me to not give in to fear at the expense of my faith in you. For this I pray. Amen.

Jesus

ASKS YOU

" What do you want me to do for you?"

³⁵As he approached Jericho, a blind man was sitting by the roadside begging. ³⁶When he heard a crowd going by, he asked what was happening. ³⁷They told him, "Jesus of Nazareth is passing by." ³⁸Then he shouted, "Jesus, Son of David, have mercy on me!" . . . ⁴⁰Jesus stood still and ordered the man to be brought to him; and when he came near, he asked him, ⁴¹**"What do you want me to do for you?"** He said, "Lord, let me see again." ⁴²Jesus said to him, "Receive your sight; your faith has saved you."

—Luke 18:35–42

Search Your Mind

What do you want Jesus to do for you today? That's quite a question. Let's say that you could ask Jesus for anything, but only one thing. What one thing would you ask Jesus to do for you? Do you suffer from a "blindness" in your life? Do you fail to see something in your life that you ought to be seeing? Perhaps you need to ask Jesus for the same thing the blind man asked for— eyes to see!

Hear Your Tradition

"God is the Father Almighty, who reveals his fatherly love by the way he takes care of our needs and by his infinite mercy, freely forgiving sins."[109] (Adapted from *CCC*, no. 270)

Commit Your Spirit

Each of us has blind spots. We fail to see things we need to see, sometimes things in ourselves, such as selfishness. We fail to see things in others, like their spiritual or material needs. We fail to see things in the world that need changing, for example, violence. Name one blind spot in yourself. Name one blind spot you have toward the needs of others. Name one blind spot you have toward the needs of the world.

Pray Your Heart

Lord, have mercy on me. You ask me, "What do you want me to do for you?" I pray that you remove the blind spots that I find in myself, in my actions and words toward others, and in my service to the world. Today help me to see the blindness in myself, in my actions to-ward others, and in my service to the world. Help me to see with the eyes of faith so that your will may be done. In your Son's name I pray. Amen.

Jesus

"What does it profit them if they gain the whole world, but lose . . . themselves?"

[23]Then he said to them all, "If any want to become my followers, let them deny themselves and take up their cross daily and follow me. [24]For those who want to save their life will lose it, and those who lose their life for my sake will save it. [25]**What does it profit them if they gain the whole world, but lose** or forfeit **themselves?** [26]Those who are ashamed of me and of my words, of them the Son of Man will be ashamed when he comes in his glory and the glory of the Father and of the holy angels."

—Luke 9:23–26

Search Your Mind

Do you think you would have greater happiness in your life if *a)* you had anything and everything in the world that money could buy, or *b)* you knew that people loved you, and you loved them in return?

This Scripture passage reminds us that we are confronted with a variety of competing values in life. We are bombarded with messages that say if we work out and develop a great body, fill our life with all the things money can buy, wear the right clothes, smell a certain way, look a certain way, and so on, then our life will be great, satisfying, and meaningful. You may have already figured out that these messages are often empty promises. These things can bring a sense of happiness, but for just a short time. It's a happiness that ultimately doesn't last.

Jesus shows us that love is the only thing that brings us happiness that lasts forever. Although some earthly things can bring temporary happiness, it is only in following Christ that we will find happiness that is eternal.

Hear Your Tradition

Taking up one's cross every day is the path to conversion, which "is accomplished in daily life by gestures of reconciliation, concern for the poor, the exercise and defense of justice and right,[33] by the admission of faults . . . , examination of conscience, spiritual direction, acceptance of suffering" (*CCC*, no. 1435).

Commit Your Spirit

In the next week, contact at least three organizations in your town that need volunteers. Choose one, and decide what priorities you need to rearrange so that you can commit to this volunteer project.

Each day after you are done with your volunteer project, think about how you feel, especially after giving up time that you otherwise would have spent on your own needs or wishes.

Pray Your Heart

Lord, help me gain life by giving of my own life in service to others, just as you did. Grant me the strength of your Spirit to consider other people's needs before my own needs. Amen.

Jesus

ASKS YOU

" What were you arguing about on the way?"

³³Then they came to Capernaum; and when he was in the house he asked them, **"What were you arguing about on the way?"** ³⁴But they were silent, for on the way they had argued with one another who was the greatest. ³⁵He sat down, called the twelve, and said to them, "Whoever wants to be first must be last of all and servant of all."

—Mark 9:33–35

Search Your Mind

Have you ever argued with others about who was the best at something? Have you ever thought that you were better than someone else? Pride, ego, arrogance—these are earthly, human concerns. For some reason people feel a need to compare themselves with others in an attempt to feel good about themselves. You might be the best runner on the track team, but if you don't have care, concern, and respect in your heart for your teammates and opponents, then what use is the gift? If Jesus had a bedroom, maybe it would be filled with a trophy or two for "most amazing carpenter," but he would probably have a whole bunch of awards recognizing him for all the good he did for others out of love for them.

Hear Your Tradition

"Christ died out of love for us. . . . The Lord asks us to love as he does, even our *enemies,* to make ourselves the neighbor of those farthest away, and to love children and the poor as Christ himself."[101] (*CCC,* no. 1825)

Commit Your Spirit

This week practice being "last of all and servant of all." Each day and every chance you get, try some of the following ideas. Open and hold the door for others until you are the last person to go through the door. In the lunch line, let others go before you until you are the last to go through the line. When class is dismissed and everyone is scrambling to get out of the classroom, let everyone leave the room before you. At the dinner table, serve the meal to your family rather than waiting to be served. Clean the dishes without being asked to do so. Come up with your own ideas to practice being the "last of all and servant of all."

Pray Your Heart

Lord, each time I slip into thinking of myself as better than others, or more important than others, lead me to serve them instead. Amen.

Jesus

" If you lend to those from whom you hope to receive, what credit is that to you?"

³⁴**If you lend to those from whom you hope to receive, what credit is that to you?** Even sinners lend to sinners, to receive as much again. ³⁵But love your enemies, do good, and lend, expecting nothing in return. Your reward will be great, and you will be children of the Most High; for he is kind to the ungrateful and the wicked. ³⁶Be merciful, just as your Father is merciful.

—Luke 6:34–36

Search Your Mind

What do you expect in return when you lend something to another person? That's a pretty good question, isn't it? Why is it that we expect something in return when we lend, give, or do something good for others? For example, when you go out to eat with your friends, and you end up having to loan one of your friends some money because he or she doesn't have enough, you "expect" to be paid back, right? Have you ever stopped to think about why you expect to be paid back? Why can't you lend something to someone else without expecting to be paid back?

Perhaps what Jesus is teaching us through this question is that God asks us to love others, to share with others unconditionally. God is kind to everyone—the unkind and the wicked, the kind and the generous—alike. He makes no distinction, because every person deserves God's love without condition. We don't earn God's love. It's a gift, freely given. Therefore, when we lend to or do good deeds for others, we ought to do so with the attitude that it is a gift, freely given, without expecting anything in return.

Hear Your Tradition

As Christians we are called to become disciples of Christ, which demands a radical commitment: to live as Christ teaches, in word and in deed. "Words are not enough, [good] deeds are required"[263] (*CCC*, no. 546).

Commit Your Spirit

Think of five good deeds you can do for others within the next few days. Perhaps think of five people who would least expect a good deed from you. Do those five good deeds. Don't brag about it. You don't even need to tell the people that you did the good deed for them. Just do it. Expect nothing in return. See how it feels.

Pray Your Heart

Father, I thank you for your Son's example of doing good deeds for others without expecting anything in return. Thank you for the gift of unconditional love that you give to me through your Son. Help me to accept that gift from you and freely share it with others. Amen.

Jesus

"Which of these . . . was a neighbor?"

[30]Jesus replied, "A man was going down from Jerusalem to Jericho, and fell into the hands of robbers, who . . . beat him, . . . leaving him half dead. [31]Now by chance a priest was going down that road; and when he saw him, he passed by on the other side. [32]So likewise a Levite. . . . [33]But a Samaritan while traveling came near him; and when he saw him, he was moved with pity. [34]He . . . bandaged his wounds, . . . put him on his own animal, brought him to an inn, and took care of him. . . . [36]**Which of these** three, do you think, **was a neighbor** to the man who fell into the hands of the robbers?" [37]He said, "The one who showed him mercy." Jesus said to him, "Go and do likewise."

—Luke 10:30–37

Search Your Mind

We have all seen this story played out in our own life. We have seen something bad happen to another person or seen someone who was hurt in some way, and we've reacted like one of the three characters in this story.

When have you acted like the priest in this story? When have you acted like the Levite in this story? What was it inside you that caused you to respond to another's hurt as the priest or the Levite did? Was it fear? Was it an uncaring heart? Was it self-centeredness?

When have you acted like the Samaritan in this story? What was it in you that caused you to notice, stop, and tend to the hurting person with care and compassion? Why is it that sometimes we stop and care, and other times we just keep on walking?

Hear Your Tradition

God is love, the source of all love. Therefore, "love of neighbor is inseparable from love for God" (*CCC*, no. 1878). It is only by God's grace that we can follow the path of self-giving and social justice, like the good Samaritan.

Commit Your Spirit

In the course of the next week, you will surely come across a situation in which someone you know, or someone you don't know, will be in need. Commit yourself to noticing, stopping, and offering your assistance to that person.

Pray Your Heart

Loving God, at times I have been blind to the needs of others. Forgive me for that. Help me to notice the needs of others. Help me to act like a "neighbor," to stop and offer help to those in need. Amen.

Jesus

"Do you see this woman?"

⁴⁴Then turning toward the woman, he said to Simon, **"Do you see this woman?** I entered your house; you gave me no water for my feet, but she has bathed my feet with her tears and dried them with her hair. ⁴⁵You gave me no kiss, but from the time I came in she has not stopped kissing my feet. ⁴⁶You did not anoint my head with oil, but she has anointed my feet with ointment. ⁴⁷Therefore, I tell you, her sins, which were many, have been forgiven; hence she has shown great love. But the one to whom little is forgiven, loves little."

—Luke 7:44–47

Search Your Mind

What was the difference between Simon and the woman in this story? Imagine that you went to the house of two people you know. The first person came to the door, greeted you, offered you refreshment, spoke with you. The second person just sat on the couch in the other room and paid no attention to you. Which of these would you consider to be more of a friend?

The woman in this story welcomed Jesus, showing him kindness and hospitality. These are marks of love, and love comes from the person who welcomes Jesus into his or her heart, who has faith in Jesus. But the one whose heart has little room for the love of Jesus has little love to offer others. Part of our human condition is that we sometimes do things that hurt others. We call this sin. Sin blocks out love.

Hear Your Tradition

Making room in our heart for Jesus, as did the woman in this story, requires spiritual conversion. Conversion is a change of heart that allows us to turn our life away from sin and evil, and toward God. This change of heart is central to Christ's preaching. (See *CCC*, nos. 821, 1423, 1427, 1431)

Commit Your Spirit

How much room do you have in your heart for the love of Jesus today? What in your heart do you need to let go of in order to have a spirit of hospitality toward others? Does something in your heart need to be reconciled? Take the time today to reconcile with others any hurt you have. Tell them you are sorry. Ask for their forgiveness. Seek the sacrament of Reconciliation this week to open your heart fully, once again, to the love of Jesus.

Pray Your Heart

Father, I am sorry for the ways I have hurt others, knowingly and unknowingly. Forgive me. Grant me your mercy. Help me make room in my heart, once again, for your love. I ask this in the name of the your Son, Jesus Christ. Amen.

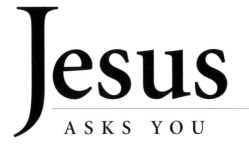

Jesus

ASKS YOU

" Why do you see the speck in your neighbor's eye, but do not notice the log in your own eye?"

[1]Do not judge, so that you may not be judged. [2]For with the judgment you make you will be judged, and the measure you give will be the measure you get. **[3]Why do you see the speck in your neighbor's eye, but do not notice the log in your own eye? [4]**Or how can you say to your neighbor, "Let me take the speck out of your eye," while the log is in your own eye? [5]You hypocrite, first take the log out of your own eye, and then you will see clearly to take the speck out of your neighbor's eye.

—Matthew 7:1–5

Search Your Mind

"Why do you see the faults in your friends, but do not notice your own faults?" How often do we do this—see the faults of others but not our own? Or we see what others are doing wrong and think that we are right.

Jesus' teaching on this subject is clear: before you concern yourself with judging others, pay attention to your own faults and make your ways blameless.

Hear Your Tradition

"We must always speak of others in an attitude that ensures respect for their reputation so that we do not 'cause them unjust injury.'[278] We become guilty of rash judgment if, 'even tacitly, [we] assume as true, without sufficient foundation, the moral fault of a neighbor.'" (Quoted and adapted from *CCC*, no. 2477)

Commit Your Spirit

Go outside and find a pebble. Place the pebble in your pocket. Each time you notice yourself finding fault with someone else, reach into your pocket and grab hold of the pebble. Let the pebble remind you to not be a hypocrite.

Pray Your Heart

Lord, help me see the faults in myself rather than judge the faults in others. At all times help me as I try to make my ways blameless. For this I pray. Amen.

Jesus

"Why do you ask me about what is good?"

[16]"Teacher, what good deed must I do to have eternal life?" [17]And [Jesus] said to him, **"Why do you ask me about what is good?** There is only one who is good. If you wish to enter into life, keep the commandments: . . . [18]You shall not murder; You shall not commit adultery; You shall not steal; You shall not bear false witness; [19]Honor your father and mother; also, You shall love your neighbor as yourself." [20]The young man said to him, "I have kept all these; what do I still lack?" [21]Jesus said to him, "If you wish to be perfect, go, sell your possessions, and give the money to the poor, and you will have treasure in heaven; then come, follow me." [22]When the young man heard this word, he went away grieving, for he had many possessions.

—Matthew 19:16–22

Search Your Mind

If you were the young man in this story, what would you have done? Would you have gone home, sold all your possessions, and given all the money to the poor?

Interestingly you never hear whether the young man in the story actually did do as Jesus asked him. You just know that he went away grieving, sad, because he had many possessions. Why do you think he was so sad? Remember, the question he asked Jesus was, "What good deed must I do to have eternal life?" He was a young man who had all kinds of possessions, but he wasn't happy! Strange, don't you think? Or perhaps you can relate to the young man's question. Do you sometimes accumulate all kinds of things that you think will make you happy, only to discover that you still seem to be missing something in your life? What Jesus teaches the young man in this story is that real happiness comes from living your life the way God intends: by living the Commandments. It's the way you live your life that matters, not the things you accumulate. True joy and fulfillment come from following Jesus, living your life as Jesus did.

Hear Your Tradition

"Following Jesus Christ involves keeping the Commandments" (*CCC*, no. 2053). As he called the rich young man, Jesus also calls us to lives of obedience to and observance of the Commandments, joined with a detachment from worldly things.

Commit Your Spirit

Do a little experiment this week. No doubt, in the course of the week, you will have the desire to buy something for yourself that you really don't need. When you notice that desire rising in you, stop and ask yourself this question: "In the time I would spend going out and buying something for myself, what is one thing I could do instead to bring joy to another person's life?" Then, do that. See what you learn from the experience.

Pray Your Heart

Lord, it is so hard to resist all the advertisements and messages in our society that tell me I will be happy if I buy this, that, or the other thing. I know that true happiness comes from following your way. Help me this week to resist the messages that compete with the message you offer. Amen.

Jesus

ASKS YOU

"Who will give you what
is your own?"

¹²And if you have not been faithful with
what belongs to another, **who will give you
what is your own?** ¹³No slave can serve two
masters; for a slave will either hate the one
and love the other, or be devoted to the one
and despise the other. You cannot serve
God and wealth.

—Luke 16:12–13

Search Your Mind

This is a question about faithfulness, and in particular about being faithful to helping others obtain what they need. In this Scripture passage, the main character is torn between being faithful to someone else, the rich man, and looking after only his own gain. Yet service of God requires us to share our goods with those who are needy. We must choose either selfishness or faithfulness to God's will, which requires that we freely share our wealth with those who are in need.

Hear Your Tradition

"[Throughout our lives God] invites us to purify our hearts of bad instincts and to seek the love of God above all else. [God] teaches us that true happiness is not found in riches or well-being, in human fame or power, or in any human achievement—however beneficial it may be—such as science, technology, and art, or indeed in any creature, but in God alone, the source of every good and of all love." (*CCC*, no. 1723)

Commit Your Spirit

Notice that when you feel the urge to buy something, it is sometimes a craving to fill an emotional gap in your life. You may think that if you buy something, it will make you happy. But God alone brings real happiness to your life.

Cut out a piece of paper about the size of a driver's license. On it write, "Ask yourself!" Place the piece of paper in your wallet or purse, or wherever you keep your money. Each time you go to buy something, pull out the piece of paper first and ask yourself, "Am I buying this to get a feeling that I know only

God can give me?" Then, decide if you really want to buy the thing you were considering.

Pray Your Heart

Lord, I desire to serve you. Help me to stop each time I begin to put my trust in something else, so that I may recommit myself to your will. Amen.

Jesus

"What do you think?"

²⁸**"What do you think?** A man had two sons; he went to the first and said, 'Son, go and work in the vineyard today.' ²⁹He answered, 'I will not'; but later he changed his mind and went. ³⁰The father went to the second and said the same; and he answered, 'I go, sir'; but he did not go. ³¹Which of the two did the will of his father?" They said, "The first." Jesus said to them, "Truly I tell you, the tax collectors and the prostitutes are going into the kingdom of God ahead of you. ³²For John came to you in the way of righteousness and you did not believe him, but the tax collectors and the prostitutes believed him; and even after you saw it, you did not change your minds and believe him."

—Matthew 21:28–32

Search Your Mind

What do you think is the difference between the two sons? The first one said no, but then obeyed. The second one said yes, but disobeyed. Which of them is more faithful to his father? This is a story about conversion, a change of heart and mind. The first son had a conversion. His heart and mind changed, and he did the will of his father. The second son did not.

Hear Your Tradition

"Jesus' invitation to enter his kingdom comes in the form of *parables,* a characteristic feature of his teaching.[261] Through his parables he invites people to the feast of the kingdom, but he also asks for a radical choice: to gain the kingdom, one must give everything.[262] Words are not enough; deeds are required."[263] (*CCC,* no. 546)

Commit Your Spirit

This week you will face moments when you will be tempted to not follow through on a commitment you made to someone. When you become aware of that temptation, stop and ask yourself whether God desires you to act like the first son or the second son. Then, commit to acting like the first son: be faithful to your commitment to others.

Pray Your Heart

Lord, sometimes I act like the first son and sometimes I act like the second son. Help me, when I am tempted to act like the second son, to act instead like the first son. Help me to turn my heart and mind to your will. Amen.

Jesus

" Are you envious because I am generous?"

¹For the kingdom of heaven is like a land-owner who went out early in the morning to hire laborers for his vineyard. ⁹When those hired about five o'clock came, each of them received the usual daily wage. ¹⁰Now when the first came, they thought they would receive more; but each of them also received the usual daily wage. ¹¹. . . They grumbled, . . . ¹²saying, "These last worked only one hour, and you have made them equal to us who have borne the bur-den of the day." . . . ¹³But he replied . . . , "Friend, I am doing you no wrong; did you not agree with me for the usual daily wage? ¹⁴Take what belongs to you and go. . . . ¹⁵Am I not allowed to do what I choose with what belongs to me? Or **are you envi-ous because I am generous?**"

—Matthew 20:1,9–15

Search Your Mind

How would you feel if you were one of the laborers who worked all day and got the same wage as the one who worked only one hour? Would you be angry, or would you be happy with what you received? This teaching of Jesus reveals God's generosity. God's sense of fairness stems from generosity. So why do we feel envious when someone is equally generous to all?

Hear Your Tradition

First of all, Christians are obliged "to practice generosity, kindness, and sharing of goods" (*CCC*, no. 1937). Yet at times we fail in our practice of generosity, and envy creeps into our heart. "The tenth commandment requires that *envy* be banished from the human heart" (no. 2538). Envy refers to the feeling of "sadness at the sight of another's goods and the immoderate desire to acquire them for oneself, even unjustly" (no. 2539).

Commit Your Spirit

Listen today and throughout the week for all the times when you or your friends say, "It's not fair." When you hear those words spoken, pause and ask yourself, "Is this being said out of envy?" If so, what might you be able to do to turn this situation from one of envy to one of appreciating the generosity shown to you or the other person?

Pray Your Heart

Lord, when envy creeps into my feelings and thoughts, help me to pause and be mindful of the generosity shown to me. Help me to be thankful for the kindness offered to me. For this I pray. Amen.

Jesus

"And can any of you by worrying add a single hour to your span of life?"

[27]**And can any of you by worrying add a single hour to your span of life?** . . . Do not worry, saying, "What will we eat?" or "What will we drink?" or "What will we wear?" [32]For it is the Gentiles who strive for all these things; and indeed your heavenly Father knows that you need all these things. [33]But strive first for the kingdom of God and his righteousness, and all these things will be given to you as well.

[34]So do not worry about tomorrow, for tomorrow will bring worries of its own. Today's trouble is enough for today.

—Matthew 6:27–34

Search Your Mind

What is it that you most worry about? Do you worry about your clothing? Do you worry about how others might judge your appearance? Do you worry about who will like you or who won't? What about your grades—do you worry about them? Do you worry about how well you're doing in after-school activities? We worry a lot, don't we?

Perhaps we have no greater modern example of what Jesus is telling us in this story than the life of Mother Teresa of Calcutta. She never worried about having enough money to do her work among poor people. Instead she stayed focused on doing the work of Christ, and in doing so she had all that she needed to tend to the needs of poor people. What use would it have been for her to worry?

Hear Your Tradition

"God the Father gives us life and gives us the nourishment life requires—'all appropriate goods and blessings, both material and spiritual.' In his Sermon on the Mount, Jesus insists on our trust in God the Father, and in his providence. Jesus invites us to accept relief from our 'nagging worry and preoccupation,' to surrender our worries in trust to God." (Quoted and adapted from *CCC*, no. 2830)

Commit Your Spirit

Get a tin can and place it on your dresser. On the outside of the can, affix a label that reads: "Warning! Worries Inside." Now get some scraps of paper and a pen or pencil. Each day, as you become aware of any worries you have, write them down on the slip of paper and place them in the can. Once a week take your worry can and toss those slips of paper in the recycling bin.

Pray Your Heart

Father, I know that you will provide what I need this day. Help me to not worry, but to turn that energy toward doing your will. Rather than worry, teach me to trust in you and to serve others out of love. I pray this in the name of the Father, and of the Son, and of the Holy Spirit. Amen.

Jesus

"Who is my mother, and
who are my brothers?"

⁴⁶While he was still speaking to the crowds,
his mother and his brothers were standing
outside, wanting to speak to him. ⁴⁷Some-
one told him, "Look, your mother and your
brothers are standing outside, wanting to
speak to you." ⁴⁸But to the one who had
told him this, Jesus replied, **"Who is my
mother, and who are my brothers?"** ⁴⁹And
pointing to his disciples, he said, "Here are
my mother and my brothers! ⁵⁰For whoever
does the will of my Father in heaven is my
brother and sister and mother."

—Matthew 12:46–50

Search Your Mind

Who do you consider to be your brother, your sister, and your mother? Jesus says, "Whoever does the will of my Father in heaven is my brother and sister and mother." In addressing youth at World Youth Day XII, Pope John Paul II told the world's young people something very similar. He said, "*Jesus is living next to you,* in the brothers and sisters with whom you share your daily existence." How would your daily life be different if you believed that every person you met who was doing the will of God was your brother, sister, and mother?

Hear Your Tradition

Jesus' true family was made up of those who gathered around him and listened as he taught them "a new 'way of acting' and a prayer of their own"[167] (*CCC*, no. 764). "Becoming a disciple of Jesus means accepting the invitation to belong to *God's family,* to live in conformity with His way of life" (no. 2233).

Commit Your Spirit

This Sunday when you attend Mass, look around the congregation. Visualize in your mind that everyone gathered in the church is your brother, sister, and mother. When you offer the sign of peace to those around you, say these words: "Peace be with you, brother/sister."

Pray Your Heart

Lord, to be part of your family is so amazing. It is mind-boggling to think that all those who believe in you and do your will are my brothers and sisters. Thank you for the gift of such a wonderful family. Grant that we may all get along as brothers and sisters in Christ. Amen.

Jesus

"Is there anyone among you who, if your child asks for bread, will give a stone?"

[7]Ask, and it will be given you; search, and you will find; knock, and the door will be opened for you. [8]For everyone who asks receives, and everyone who searches finds, and for everyone who knocks, the door will be opened. [9]**Is there anyone among you who, if your child asks for bread, will give a stone?** . . . [11]If you then, who are evil, know how to give good gifts to your children, how much more will your Father in heaven give good things to those who ask him!

—Matthew 7:7–11

Search Your Mind

If you were a parent and your child asked you for bread, would you give her or him a stone instead? Realize that asking for bread is a request for something that sustains life. Bread nourishes our body, it helps us think and move and breathe, it keeps us alive. God, our Father in heaven, sustains us and gives us life, too. That is why when we search for God, when we knock on his door and ask for the "bread of life," God will always give it to us. God the Father, with his Son, Jesus Christ, freely and always offers us the gift of his Spirit, which is the spiritual bread of life that we all need to live.

Hear Your Tradition

"Once committed to conversion, the heart learns to pray in *faith*." Faith is an adherence to God to trust "beyond what we feel and understand." Christ gives us access to God, the Father, therefore "he can ask us to 'seek' and to 'knock,' since he himself is the door and the way."[65] (Quoted and adapted from *CCC*, no. 2609)

Commit Your Spirit

This week listen for the times when you hear someone ask for something that you can give. Maybe you'll hear someone at your lunch table ask for one of your French fries. Give that person some fries. Maybe you'll hear someone ask for a drink of water. Give that person a drink of water. Maybe you'll hear someone say they need a hug. Give that person a hug. Act like God wants you and asks you to act—do good things for those who ask, just as God gives good gifts to anyone who asks.

Pray Your Heart

Dear Lord, open my ears this week so that I can hear when others ask for good gifts. Help me to be more generous in giving good gifts. I pray for this in the name of the Father, and of the Son, and of the Holy Spirit. Amen.

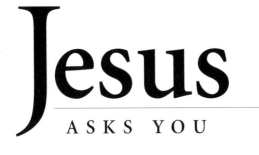

Jesus

ASKS YOU

"Does he not . . . go in search of the one that went astray?"

¹²What do you think? If a shepherd has a hundred sheep, and one of them has gone astray, **does he not** leave the ninety-nine on the mountains and **go in search of the one that went astray?** ¹³And if he finds it, truly I tell you, he rejoices over it more than over the ninety-nine that never went astray. ¹⁴So it is not the will of your Father in heaven that one of these little ones should be lost.

—Matthew 18:12–14

Search Your Mind

So how would you answer this question? Would you leave the ninety-nine and go in search of the one that went astray? In this passage Jesus gives testament to the depth of God's love for every one of his people. Not a single person is ever out of God's concern. He looks after every last one of us with love, and asks us to do the same.

Hear Your Tradition

"At the end of the parable of the lost sheep Jesus recalled that God's love excludes no one. . . . The Church, following the apostles, teaches that Christ died for all [people] without exception: 'There is not, never has been, and never will be a single human being for whom Christ did not suffer.'"[412] (*CCC*, no. 605)

Commit Your Spirit

My guess is that in your school cafeteria, 99 percent of the students sit with friends or people they know, but at least 1 percent sit alone. Perhaps they feel that they have no friends, or perhaps they are new to the school and do not know anyone yet. Today look for a student who is sitting alone. Take your lunch and ask him or her if you can sit down and eat lunch together. Introduce yourself and get to know that student a bit. Would not Jesus do the same?

Pray Your Heart

Lord, grant me the courage to reach out to someone whom I ordinarily would not talk to, not to mention eat lunch with. Help me to live out the will of your Father, who asks that not "one of these . . . should be lost." For this I pray. Amen.

Jesus

"What are you arguing about with them?"

[14]When they came to the disciples, they saw a great crowd around them, and some scribes arguing with them. [15]When the whole crowd saw him, they were immediately overcome with awe. . . . [16]He asked them, **"What are you arguing about with them?"** [17]Someone from the crowd answered him, "Teacher, I brought you my son; he has a spirit that makes him unable to speak; [18]. . . and he foams and grinds his teeth and becomes rigid; and I asked your disciples to cast it, but they could not do so." [19]He answered them, "You faithless generation, how much longer must I be among you? How much longer must I put up with you? Bring him to me."

—Mark 9:14–19

Search Your Mind

Have you ever found yourself arguing with someone about a difference of opinion? The disciples were arguing with scribes in the crowd about whether or not Jesus could heal a young man. Jesus was disturbed by their arguing because he recognized that they had a lack of faith in the power of God. This question confronts you with the need to ask yourself whether or not you find yourself arguing because of a lack of belief or trust in God's power.

Hear Your Tradition

"The disciple of Christ must not only keep the faith and live on it, but also profess it, confidently bear witness to it, and spread it. . . . Service of and witness to the faith are necessary for salvation." (*CCC*, no. 1816)

Commit Your Spirit

Asking questions about your faith in God is normal. You may not know who you can talk to about your questions, so here's an idea. Write down on a piece of paper or on this page one question you have about your faith. Schedule a time this week to meet with your church's pastor, deacon, youth minister, religion teacher, or the like, and tell her or him that you would like to talk about your question. Talk through your question with this person and ask her or him to pray for you, that you will come to a clearer and more personal answer to your question. After having this conversation, go back to the piece of paper on which you wrote your question. Write down what you learned or how your thinking or feelings have changed since having the conversation.

Pray Your Heart

Lord, when I have questions of faith, help me to listen for your words in my heart, in my mind, and in my soul, and to speak your words from my lips. Help me to trust in you and have faith in you always. I pray for this in the name of the Father, and of the Son, and of the Holy Spirit. Amen.

Jesus

ASKS YOU

"Who touched me?"

⁴⁵Then Jesus asked, **"Who touched me?"**
When all denied it, Peter said, "Master, the crowds surround you and press in on you."
⁴⁶But Jesus said, "Someone touched me; for I noticed that power had gone out from me." ⁴⁷When the woman saw that she could not remain hidden, she came trembling; and falling down before him, she declared in the presence of all the people why she had touched him, and how she had been immediately healed. ⁴⁸He said to her, "Daughter, your faith has made you well; go in peace."

—Luke 8:45–48

Search Your Mind

One question that may come to mind after reading this passage is, "Are you ever afraid to step in front of the 'crowd' to admit your faith in Christ?" Another question that may come to mind is, "Are you ever afraid to let God know that you believe in him?" The woman came trembling before Jesus, not before others. You can almost picture this scene in your head, can't you? Here is a woman, healed by the touch of Jesus, trembling to admit publicly that she believes in the Lord, even in his very presence. Yet once she publicly admits her faith, Jesus commends her for it and sends her forth in peace.

Hear Your Tradition

"A holy fear of God is one of the gifts of the Holy Spirit" (based on *CCC*, no. 1041). This gift of the Spirit is "first of all a work of the grace of God who makes our hearts return to him" so that we can conform our lives to his will (*CCC*, no. 1432).

Commit Your Spirit

First this week pay attention to the times when you are aware of fearing to come before the Lord in prayer. Remember that the Lord welcomes all who turn to him. Also this week think of something you can do to publicly show that you believe in Jesus. Perhaps you could wear a cross on the outside of your clothing, or you could carry your Bible to school to let it be known that you read the word of God. Perhaps you can think of something else. Beware that these outward signs become empty if your words and deeds don't reflect what you say you believe! So don't just say, "I believe"—act accordingly.

Pray Your Heart

Lord, give me the courage to come before you and be reconciled with you. Help me also to publicly admit my belief in you. Let me do so not as boasting, but so that others may come to know you and have faith in you, too. For this I pray in your name. Amen.

Jesus

" How long has this been happening to him?"

²⁰And they brought the boy to him. When the spirit saw him, immediately it convulsed the boy, and he fell on the ground and rolled about, foaming at the mouth. ²¹Jesus asked the father, **"How long has this been happening to him?"** And he said, "From childhood. ²²It has often cast him into the fire and into the water, to destroy him; but if you are able to do anything, have pity on us and help us." ²³Jesus said to him, "If you are able!—All things can be done for the one who believes." ²⁴Immediately the father of the child cried out, "I believe; help my unbelief!"

—Mark 9:20–24

Search Your Mind

Another version of the question Jesus asks is, "Do you believe that all things are possible for the one who believes in God?" . . . Jesus knows we will always be people who both believe and disbelieve at the same time? Is this why the father of the child cried out, "I believe; help my unbelief"? As Christians we believe in Christ Jesus, and yet we know that we do not believe as fully as we are able. That is, we have moments in which we believe, but we struggle to fully believe in Jesus and his power.

Hear Your Tradition

"Belief as a personal act is the total adherence to God, who reveals himself in deed and word through Jesus Christ" (based on *CCC*, no. 176). "Faith is a . . . gift from God. In order to believe, [we] need the interior helps of the Holy Spirit" (*CCC*, no. 179).

Commit Your Spirit

Take an opportunity this week to seek the sacrament of Reconciliation. There is perhaps no more powerful way to place our unbelief before the Lord than to seek a deeper faith and openness of heart through the sacraments. After attending the sacrament of Reconciliation, pray the words of the father in this Scripture story, "Lord, I believe; help my unbelief!"

Pray Your Heart

Lord, I do believe in you, but at times I am aware that my faith is not complete. Help me to know that even in those moments, you are present. I know that because you are present even in my unbelief, I can grow into a deeper belief in you. Help my unbelief today and always. Amen.

Jesus

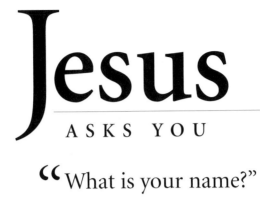

ASKS YOU

" What is your name?"

⁹Then Jesus asked him, **"What is your name?"** He replied, "My name is Legion; for we are many." . . . ¹³And the unclean spirits came out and entered the swine; and the herd, numbering about two thousand, rushed down the steep bank into the sea, and were drowned in the sea.

¹⁹Jesus . . . said to him, "Go home to your friends, and tell them how much the Lord has done for you, and what mercy he has shown you." ²⁰And he went away and began to proclaim in the Decapolis how much Jesus had done for him; and everyone was amazed.

—Mark 5:9–13,19–20

Search Your Mind

Jesus encountered a man possessed by a demon. After hearing the name of the demon, Jesus drove it out of the man and opened up room in his heart, mind, and whole being for the Lord. When Jesus asks us, "What is your name?" we are likely not possessed by a demon and so would not answer, "Legion." However, this question allows us to consider what name we would give to ourselves. How we name ourselves is an indication of what has power over us. That is, if Jesus were to ask you, "What is your name?" would you answer, "I am a Christian" or "I am a believer in the Lord"?

In the second part of this passage, Jesus said to the formerly demon-possessed man, the man who now had a heart and mind freed for loving the Lord, to consider all the ways in which the Lord had been good and merciful in his life. If you were asked this question, "How much has Jesus done for you?" how would you even begin to answer it? The point Jesus makes is that he is the source of all that is good in your life. He is the one whose mercy is always available, despite sin in your life or blindness to that which is good.

Hear Your Tradition

"Jesus performed acts, such as pardoning sins, that manifested him to be the Savior God himself (cf. *Jn* 5:16–18). Certain Jews, who did not recognize God made man (cf. *Jn* 1:14), saw in him only a man who made himself God (*Jn* 10:33), and judged him as a blasphemer." (*CCC*, no. 594)

Commit Your Spirit

In this Scripture account, Jesus tells the man, formerly known as Legion, to go home and tell all his friends what the Lord has done for him. What is one thing you are grateful for that the Lord has done for you? Now, with that in mind, go and tell three people about this one thing you are grateful for and how this thing is the result of God's goodness. Like the people in the Scripture story, those who hear of God's goodness will be amazed.

Pray Your Heart

Lord, you have shown me such mercy in my life. Thank you for all that is good in my life, which is a gift from you. I am especially grateful for [name the one thing you thought of above]. Thank you, God, for all you have done for me. I am amazed! Amen.

Jesus

"Were not ten made clean? But the other nine, where are they?"

[12]As he entered a village, ten lepers approached him. . . . [14]When he saw them, he said to them, "Go and show yourselves to the priests." And as they went, they were made clean. [15]Then one of them, when he saw that he was healed, turned back, praising God with a loud voice. [16]. . . And he was a Samaritan. [17]Then Jesus asked, **"Were not ten made clean? But the other nine, where are they?** [18]Was none of them found to return and give praise to God except this foreigner?" [19]Then he said to him, "Get up and go on your way; your faith has made you well."

—Luke 17:12–19

Search Your Mind

Jesus asks you, "Why do you not give praise to God for the good that he does in your life?" Ten were healed, but only one "turned back, praising God with a loud voice." Do you sometimes forget to give thanks to God for all that is good in your life? What do you think causes this? Is it just forgetfulness? Is it selfishness? Can you imagine giving someone a gift and her or him never thanking you in return? Have you had that experience? How does it feel? Do you think God feels the same way when you fail to thank him for the gifts he gives you each day?

Hear Your Tradition

We are to adore God by acknowledging that we would not exist but for God's goodness. "To adore God is to praise and exalt him and to humble oneself, as Mary did . . . , confessing with gratitude that he has done great things and holy is his name"[14] (*CCC*, no. 2097).

Commit Your Spirit

Write out a list today of everything you recognize as a gift in your life. Begin with the gift of waking up and having a new day of life. Then, throughout the day keep note of everything that you might ordinarily take for granted, but know that it is a gift from God. Before going to sleep, praise and thank God for all the gifts given to you this day.

Pray Your Heart

Dear God, I am so grateful for every gift, every blessing that you give to me out of your love. Thank you especially for [read from the list you made today, thanking God for each gift]. You bless me abundantly. Thank you. Amen.

Jesus

"Why are you sleeping?"

[45]When he got up from prayer, he came to the disciples and found them sleeping because of grief, [46]and he said to them, **"Why are you sleeping?** Get up and pray that you may not come into the time of trial."

—Luke 22:45–46

Search Your Mind

Do you ever find yourself sleeping when you could be or ought to be praying? How often have you intended to pray before you go to sleep at night, but end up falling asleep or doing something else instead? How often have you told yourself that you will get up early to pray before school, but end up sleeping late? Jesus is not criticizing the value of sleep, but reminding us that there are moments in life, lots of them, that call for us to pray.

Hear Your Tradition

"'[Jesus] calls his hearers to conversion and faith, but also to *watchfulness*.' In prayer, as disciples, we are to keep watch, ever attentive to Christ in memory of his first coming and in hope of his second coming.[73] 'Only by keeping watch in prayer can one avoid falling into temptation.'"[74] (Quoted and adapted from *CCC*, no. 2612)

Commit Your Spirit

Commit yourself to praying each night before you go to sleep or each morning as you wake up. Commit to ten minutes of prayer, and try the following routine: Kneel beside your bed (Have you ever noticed that it's really hard to fall asleep when kneeling? So don't lie down or sit in a comfortable chair— kneel!). Cross yourself in the name of the Father, the Son, and the Holy Spirit. Ask God for help in leading you into prayer and that your time in prayer will draw you closer to him. Read a short passage from your Bible or from a prayer book. Meditate on the words you read. Listen for what God is speaking to you in those words. Ask God to help you live the words you heard.

Pray Your Heart

Lord, help me to stay awake so that I may pray each night or each morning. In my prayer let me hear the words you speak to me so that I may live as you desire. I pray this in your Son's name, Jesus Christ, the Lord. Amen.

Jesus

"If you love those who love you, what reward do you have?"

[43]You have heard that it was said, "You shall love your neighbor and hate your enemy." [44]But I say to you, Love your enemies and pray for those who persecute you, [45]so that you may be children of your Father in heaven; for he makes his sun rise on the evil and on the good, and sends rain on the righteous and on the unrighteous. [46]For **if you love those who love you, what reward do you have?** Do not even the tax collectors do the same? [47]And if you greet only your brothers and sisters, what more are you doing than others? Do not even the Gentiles do the same?

—Matthew 5:43–47

Search Your Mind

Do I say hello only to people who say hello to me? Do I love only people who love me in return? Jesus is asking us to realize that it's fairly easy to love those who love us in return, or to associate with people whom we like, but it's much harder to love people who dislike us. It's difficult to associate with people we don't know or understand, people we think are weird or strange, right?

Love, Jesus teaches, is a gift from God that is freely given to all people, those who are good and evil, righteous and unrighteous. Just as God freely extends his love to all people, so must we, even if it is a difficult thing to do at times.

Hear Your Tradition

"The obligation to love others extends to 'those who think or act differently from us,' and forgiveness is a requirement of the Christian. Although we can hate the wrongdoing of others, we cannot harbor any hatred for another, especially our enemy." (Quoted and adapted from *CCC* no. 1933)

Commit Your Spirit

Today you will see a lot of people you don't know, people you don't ordinarily talk to. Try this: say hello to every person you walk past today. See if it doesn't bring a smile to their face. See if it doesn't make you feel a little happier yourself.

Pray Your Heart

Heavenly Father, I may not have a lot of enemies, but I certainly know some people who don't like me, and truth be told, some people I don't like. I want to pray for them today. Bless [offer the names of people who may not like you or whom you may not like]. Help me to do what you ask of me, to be kind and patient, to love and accept these people. I ask this in the name of the Father, and of the Son, and of the Holy Spirit. Amen.

Jesus

"Why are you afraid?"

^{35}On that day, when evening had come, he said to them, "Let us go across to the other side." ^{36}And leaving the crowd behind, they took him with them in the boat, just as he was. Other boats were with him. ^{37}A great windstorm arose, and the waves beat into the boat, so that the boat was already being swamped. ^{38}But he was in the stern, asleep on the cushion; and they woke him up and said to him, "Teacher, do you not care that we are perishing?" ^{39}He woke up and rebuked the wind, and said to the sea, "Peace! Be still!" Then the wind ceased, and there was a dead calm. ^{40}He said to them, **"Why are you afraid?** Have you still no faith?" ^{41}And they were filled with great awe and said to one another, "Who then is this, that even the wind and the sea obey him?"

—Mark 4:35–41

Search Your Mind

What are your fears? What is it about these things that you fear?

In this Scripture story, you read that Christ cared deeply about the fear he discovered within his disciples. He cared so much for them that when he heard their fear, he "woke up and rebuked the wind, and said to the sea, 'Peace! Be still!'" This is what Christ wants for you when you are seized with fear. He wants you to have his peace, so that your fear may be calmed.

Hear Your Tradition

"'The kingdom of God [is] righteousness and peace and joy in the Holy Spirit.'[90] The end-time in which we live is the age of the outpouring of the Spirit." (*CCC*, no. 2819)

Commit Your Spirit

Fold a sheet of paper into three sections. In the first section, write down the things you fear. In the second section, write down the reasons you fear those things. In the third section, write down what you ask of God in calming those fears.

Pray Your Heart

Lord, just as you did for the disciples on the stormy sea, please grant me peace in the times that I am overwhelmed by my fear. Amen.

Jesus

"When the Son of Man comes, will he find faith on earth?"

²[Jesus] said, "In a certain city there was a judge who neither feared God nor had respect for people. ³In that city there was a widow who kept coming to him and saying, 'Grant me justice against my opponent.' ⁴For a while he refused; but later he said to himself, ⁵'. . . I will grant her justice, so that she may not wear me out by continually coming.'" ⁶And the Lord said, "Listen to what the unjust judge says. ⁷And will not God grant justice to his chosen ones who cry to him day and night? ⁸I tell you, he will quickly grant justice to them. And yet, **when the Son of Man comes, will he find faith on earth?**"

—Luke 18:2–8

Search Your Mind

If the Lord were to appear today, would he find faith on earth? This question may be more relevant today than when Jesus first asked it of his disciples. Jesus was among them teaching the importance of praying always, of placing their hope and faith in God every moment of the day. To pray always, to not lose heart, these are the things you must learn to do as well.

Let's get a bit more personal. If Jesus were to appear today, would he find you to be a person of faith?

Hear Your Tradition

"Prayer and *Christian life* are *inseparable,* for they concern the same love" (*CCC,* no. 2745). Prayer helps us to "act habitually according to the Spirit of Christ" (no. 2752). Prayer leads us from temptation. "It is always possible to pray. It is even a vital necessity" (no. 2757).

Commit Your Spirit

Praying always doesn't necessarily mean praying out loud everywhere you go. On the other hand, praying out loud is a good discipline to help you remember to always place your trust and faith in God. Try this discipline at the start of every activity you do this week, either saying the following words privately or out loud: "Lord, grant that I may do your will now and forever."

Pray Your Heart

Lord, I want to be a person of faith. Help me during those times when my faith is weak. Teach me to pray always so that my faith is constantly placed in you. For this I pray. Amen.

Topic Index

Actions, 25, 37, 83, 86, 90, 91, 100, 107
Advertising, 52
Arguing, 31, 32, 77, 78
Belief. *See* Faith
Blamelessness, 47, 48
Blessings, 65, 94, 101
Blindness, 23, 24, 25, 41, 90
Boasting, 84
Body image, 28
Bread, 70, 71
Brothers, 67, 68, 69
Calm, 20, 103, 104, 105
Care, 24, 32, 39, 40, 43, 103, 104
Clothing, 28, 63, 64
Commandments, 49, 51
Commitment, 37, 59
Compassion, 40
Concern, 32, 75
Conversations about God. *See* Witness
Conversion, 29, 44, 57, 58, 71, 96
Courage, 76, 84
Creator God, 18
Disciples, 27, 37, 51, 67, 68, 77, 78, 104, 105, 107

Discipline, 108
Ego, 32, 34
Enemies, 33, 35, 99, 100, 101, 102
Envy, 60, 61, 62
Eternal life, 17, 29, 49, 50
Evil, 21, 44, 100
Faith, 20, 21, 22, 23, 26, 43, 53, 54, 58, 71,
    78, 79, 80, 81, 82, 84, 85, 86, 87, 92, 96,
    103, 106, 107, 108
Faithlessness, 77, 78, 85, 86, 87
Family, 67, 68, 69
Faults, 46, 47, 48
Fear, 20, 21, 22, 40, 82, 83, 103, 104, 105,
    106
Food, 63, 65, 70, 71
Forgiveness, 24, 29, 41, 42, 44, 45, 90, 100
Friends, 19, 43, 76, 91
Fulfillment, 17
Generosity, 36, 60, 61, 62, 73
Gifts, 32, 37, 69, 70, 71, 72, 73, 82, 86, 91,
    94, 100
Glory, 27
God's will, 18, 22, 26, 51, 52, 54, 56, 57, 58,
    59, 66, 67, 68, 69, 72, 74, 76, 83, 108
Good, 21, 49, 55, 90, 91, 93, 100

Good works, 32, 35, 36, 37, 38, 41, 49, 50, 58, 64, 72, 83, 86
Grace, 41, 83
Gratitude, 91, 94
Greatness, 31, 94
Happiness, 17, 28, 29, 50, 51, 52, 54, 55, 101, 104
Healing, 24, 78, 81, 82, 92, 93
Holy Spirit, 17
Hope, 107
Hospitality, 43, 44
Humility, 93
Hypocrisy, 46, 48
Injustice, 39, 40, 62
Judgments, 46, 47, 48
Justice, 25, 29, 41, 106
Kindness, 39, 43, 61, 101, 102
Kingdom of God, 57, 58, 63, 104
Life, the, 17
Loneliness, 76
Lost, the, 74, 75, 76
Love, 24, 28, 29, 32, 33, 35, 36, 37, 38, 41, 42, 43, 44, 45, 53, 55, 66, 75, 89, 94, 99, 100, 102, 107
Mass, 69
Mercy, 23, 24, 25, 35, 39, 45, 88, 90, 91

Messiah, 16
Money. *See* Wealth
Mother, 67, 68
Names, 88, 89
Needs, 25, 30
Neighbor, 33, 39, 41, 46, 47, 99
Obedience, 51, 57, 58
Parables, 58
Patience, 102
Peace, 69, 81, 82, 103, 104, 105
Poor, the, 29, 33, 49, 50, 54, 64
Possessions, 49, 50, 51, 52, 62
Power, 54, 78, 81, 86, 89
Praise, 92, 93, 94
Prayer, 71, 95, 96, 97, 98, 106, 107, 108
Presence, 82, 87
Priorities, 30
Reconciliation, 29, 44, 84, 87
Respect, 32, 47, 106
Revealed truths, 16, 17, 19, 24
Rewards, 35, 36, 37, 38, 99
Riches. *See* Wealth
Salvation, 23, 78
Savior, 17
Seeking, 70, 72, 74, 75
Self-centeredness, 40

Self-examination, 29
Selfishness, 25, 54, 93
Servant, 31, 33, 34
Service, 25, 30, 33, 39, 41, 42, 52, 53, 54, 56,
    66, 78
Sharing, 36, 37, 38, 54, 61
Sin, 42, 43, 44, 90
Sisters, 67, 68, 69
Son of God, 16, 17, 18
Son of Man, 16, 27, 106
Suffering, 29, 39, 75
Temptation, 59, 97, 107
Thanksgiving, 91, 92, 93, 94
Trials, 95
Trust, 21, 22, 56, 65, 66, 71, 78, 80, 108
Truth, the, 17
Unbelief. *See* Faithlessness
Values, 28
Violence, 25
Volunteer, 30
Wages, 60, 61
Way, the, 17
Wealth, 28, 49, 50, 51, 53, 54, 64
Witness, 19, 78, 79, 82, 83, 84, 88, 91, 94
Word of God, 17
Words, 25, 37, 58, 80, 83, 86, 97, 98
Worry, 63, 64, 65, 66

Acknowledgments

(continued from copyright page)

The scriptural passages in this book are taken from *The Catholic Youth Bible*, New Revised Standard Version, Catholic Edition. Copyright © 2000 by Saint Mary's Press. All rights reserved. Permission applied for.

The excerpts marked *CCC* are from the English translation of the *Catechism of the Catholic Church* for the United States of America, second edition. Copyright © 1994 by the United States Conference of Catholic Bishops (USCCB)—Libreria Editrice Vaticana. English translation of the *Catechism of the Catholic Church: Modifications from the Editio Typica* copyright © 1997 by the USCCB—Libreria Editrice Vaticana.

The excerpt on page 21 is from *She Said Yes: The Unlikely Martyrdom of Cassie Bernall*, by Misty Bernall (New York: Pocket Books, a division of Simon and Schuster, 1999), page ix. Copyright © 1999 by Misty Bernall.

The excerpt on page 68 is from the World Youth Day XII message of Pope John Paul II, reprinted by permission of *L'Osservatore Romano*.

Endnotes from the *Catechism of the Catholic Church*

Page 24
Endnote 109: 2 Cor. 6:18; cf. Matt. 6:32

Page 29
Endnote 33: Cf. Amos 5:24; Isa. 1:17

Page 33
Endnote 101: Cf. Matt. 5:44; Luke 10:27–37;
Mark 9:37; Matt. 25:40,45

Page 37
Endnote 263: Cf. Matt. 21:28–32

Page 47
Endnote 278: Cf. CIC, can. 220

Page 58
Endnote 261: Cf. Mark 4:33–34
Endnote 262: Cf. Matt. 13:44–45; 22:1–14
Endnote 263: Cf. Matt. 21:28–32

Page 68
Endnote 167: Cf. Matt. 5—6

Page 72
Endnote 65: Cf. Matt. 7:7–11,13–14

Page 75
Endnote 412: Council of Quiercy (853): DS 624; cf. 2 Cor. 5:15; 1 John 2:2

Page 94
Endnote 14: Cf. Luke 1:46–49

Pages 96–97
Endnote 73: Cf. Mark 13; Luke 21:34–36
Endnote 74: Cf. Luke 22:40,46

Page 104
Endnote 90: Rom. 14:17

Notes

Notes

Notes

About the Author

John M. Vitek currently serves as president and chief operating officer of Saint Mary's Press. He is the author of *My Dear Young Friends: Pope John Paul II Speaks to Teens on Life, Love, and Courage* (Winona, MN: Saint Mary's Press, 2001), and *A Companion Way: Mentoring Youth in Searching Faith* (Winona, MN: Saint Mary's Press, 1993). When he is not at work, you will find John working on the family hobby farm, playing with his children, restoring turn-of-the-century barns, raising llamas and goats, or paddling a whitewater river in some remote wilderness of the United States.